SHOCKING CHRISTMAS FACTS FOR KIDS

FUN HOLIDAY TRIVIA AND SURPRISING STORIES FROM AROUND THE WORLD

ISBN 978-1-7360152-3-0

SME PUBLISHING
Copyright © 2025 by P. J. Starr
ALL RIGHTS RESERVED
Cover and interior design by P. J. Starr
Some illustrations and photographs sourced from Canva Pro, used under license.

NO PART OF THIS PUBLICATION MAY BE REPRODUCED IN WHOLE OR IN PART, OR STORED IN A RETRIEVAL SYSTEM, OR TRANSMITTED IN ANY FORM OR BY ANY MEANS, ELECTRONIC, MECHANICAL, PHOTOCOPYING, RECORDING, OR OTHERWISE, WITHOUT THE WRITTEN PERMISSION OF THE PUBLISHER/AUTHOR.

SHOCKING CHRISTMAS FACTS FOR KIDS

FUN HOLIDAY TRIVIA AND SURPRISING STORIES FROM AROUND THE WORLD

P. J. Starr
SME Publishing

FUN FACT BOOKS for Kids

This book belongs to

GET READY TO JINGLE YOUR BRAIN!

Did you know that Christmas trees used to be hung upside down? Or that eggnog was a pirate drink?

In this book, you'll discover all kinds of weird and wonderful things about reindeer, stockings, Santa, holiday food, and _snow_ much more.

COME ON!
LET'S UNWRAP THESE FUN FACTS TOGETHER!

CHRISTMAS SONGS

"Jingle Bells" was originally a Thanksgiving song!

It was first titled "One Horse Open Sleigh."

I'm not kidding.

The song "The Twelve Days of Christmas" actually refers to the 12 days <u>after</u> December 25, leading up to January 6.

A reindeer's nose really does turn red sometimes! (Just like Rudolph!)

Cold weather can create more blood flow to their noses to keep them warm.

"FEATHER TREES"

The tradition of decorating trees likely began in Germany over 400 years ago.

THE FIRST ARTIFICIAL CHRISTMAS TREES WERE MADE IN GERMANY... OUT OF GOOSE FEATHERS DYED GREEN!

What!

In the groovy 1960s, people in America loved futuristic things.

So they made Christmas trees out of shiny aluminum instead of regular green branches.

In the early days, people decorated trees with apples, nuts, and candles instead of ornaments.

It takes about 6-12 years to grow a Christmas tree.

Electric Christmas lights were invented in 1882 by Edward Johnson, who was a friend and business partner of Thomas Edison.

Do you help decorate your tree?

TINSEL WAS ORIGINALLY MADE FROM REAL SILVER, WHICH MADE TREES SPARKLE BUT WAS ALSO VERY EXPENSIVE.

Plus, it tarnished too easily!

Tinsel was first used to adorn sculptures before it became a popular decoration for Christmas trees.

Traditionally, candy canes taste like peppermint, but now you can get all kinds of flavors.
Even really weird ones like bacon or mac & cheese!

Shhh...

It's true!

Candy canes were invented to keep children quiet during long church services! The shape was said to represent a shepherd's staff.

Santa has many names around the world...

Do you have a nickname?

United Kingdom: Father Christmas
Netherlands: Saint Nicholas (SinterKlaas)
France Père Noël
Russia: Grandfather Frost
Spain: Papa Noel
Germany: Christmas Man

It's believed that "Kris Kringle" came from a mix-up between two totally different Christmas traditions! It's possibly a misheard version of Christkindl.

In Italy, gifts are delivered by La Befana, a friendly witch who rides a broomstick instead of a sleigh.

In places like Switzerland and Germany, some kids get gifts from Christkindl, who is a kind angel.

STOCKINGS

The tradition of Christmas stockings comes from the legend of Saint Nicholas, a kind man who secretly tossed bags of gold into the stockings of three poor sisters so they could marry. The stockings had been hung by the fire to dry. That's why we still hang them near the fireplace today!

Oranges (or tangerines) in stockings symbolize the bags of gold from the Saint Nicholas story. That's why your grandparents might still put an orange in the toe!

Coal in a stocking was a warning gift for naughty kids, but in Italy, it's actually sweet! Kids get "carbone dolce," a black candy shaped like coal

The world's largest Christmas stocking was big enough to hold a small airplane!

In the Netherlands, children leave out wooden clogs instead of stockings

SNOW CAN BE PINK, ORANGE, OR GREEN DEPENDING ON CERTAIN KINDS OF ALGAE THAT LIVE IN IT!

Pink snow is sometimes called "watermelon snow."

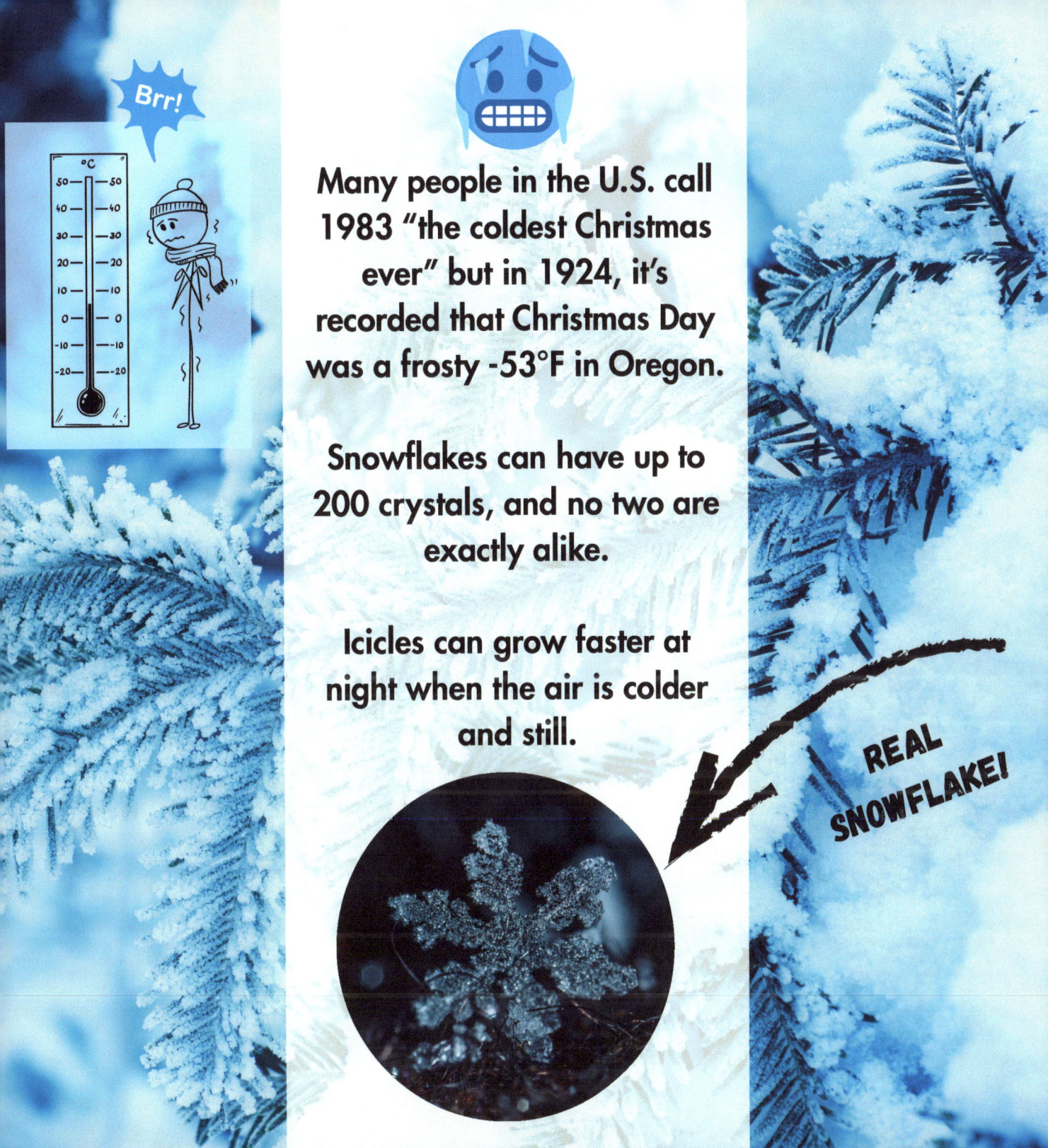

Many people in the U.S. call 1983 "the coldest Christmas ever" but in 1924, it's recorded that Christmas Day was a frosty -53°F in Oregon.

Snowflakes can have up to 200 crystals, and no two are exactly alike.

Icicles can grow faster at night when the air is colder and still.

REAL SNOWFLAKE!

Brr!

REINDEER ARE REAL!
THEY'RE CALLED CARIBOU
IN NORTH AMERICA.

Santa's reindeer are most likely female. While both male and female reindeer grow antlers, males lose theirs before Christmas. Females keep theirs through winter!

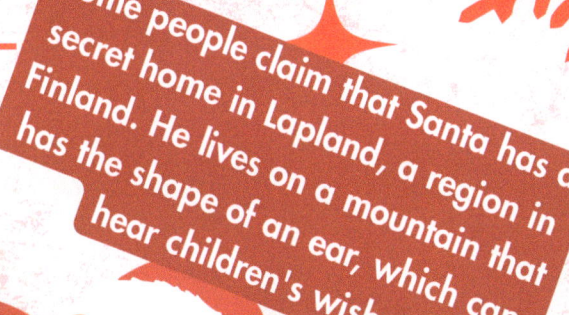

Some people claim that Santa has a secret home in Lapland, a region in Finland. He lives on a mountain that has the shape of an ear, which can hear children's wishes

HO HO HO

The North Pole has 6 months of continuous daylight and 6 months of continuous darkness.

In Japan, many people eat KFC on Christmas Day. It's such a big deal that you have to order weeks – or months! – in advance.

In Australia, Christmas falls in the summer, so families there often go to the beach or have a pool party to celebrate the holiday.

The Phillipines have the longest Christmas season in the world! It starts in September and lasts until January.

THAT'S 4 MONTHS!

DO YOU LEAVE COOKIES AND MILK FOR SANTA? SOME PLACES LEAVE SOMETHING ELSE!

United Kingdom: mince pies, a small glass of sherry or brandy, plus a carrot for Rudolph!

Finland: porridge and butter

Ireland: Guinness or milk and Christmas pudding

Australia: beer or lemonade and a slice of fruitcake or biscuits (cookies)

New Zealand: pineapple chunks or pavlova plus hay for the reindeer

Sweden: coffee to help Santa stay awake!

Marshmallows weren't always fluffy little treats. The root of the marsh mallow plant was first used as medicine!

IN ITALY, THEY MAKE HOT CHOCOLATE SO THICK YOU CAN EAT IT WITH A SPOON!

The word "cocoa" comes from a spelling mistake! A long time ago early English traders wrote "cacao" wrong, but the incorrect version stayed around.

Many people like to add peppermint, cinnamon, or whipped cream to their hot chocolate. In Mexico, sometimes chili powder is added!

Yum!

What do you like to put in your hot chocolate?

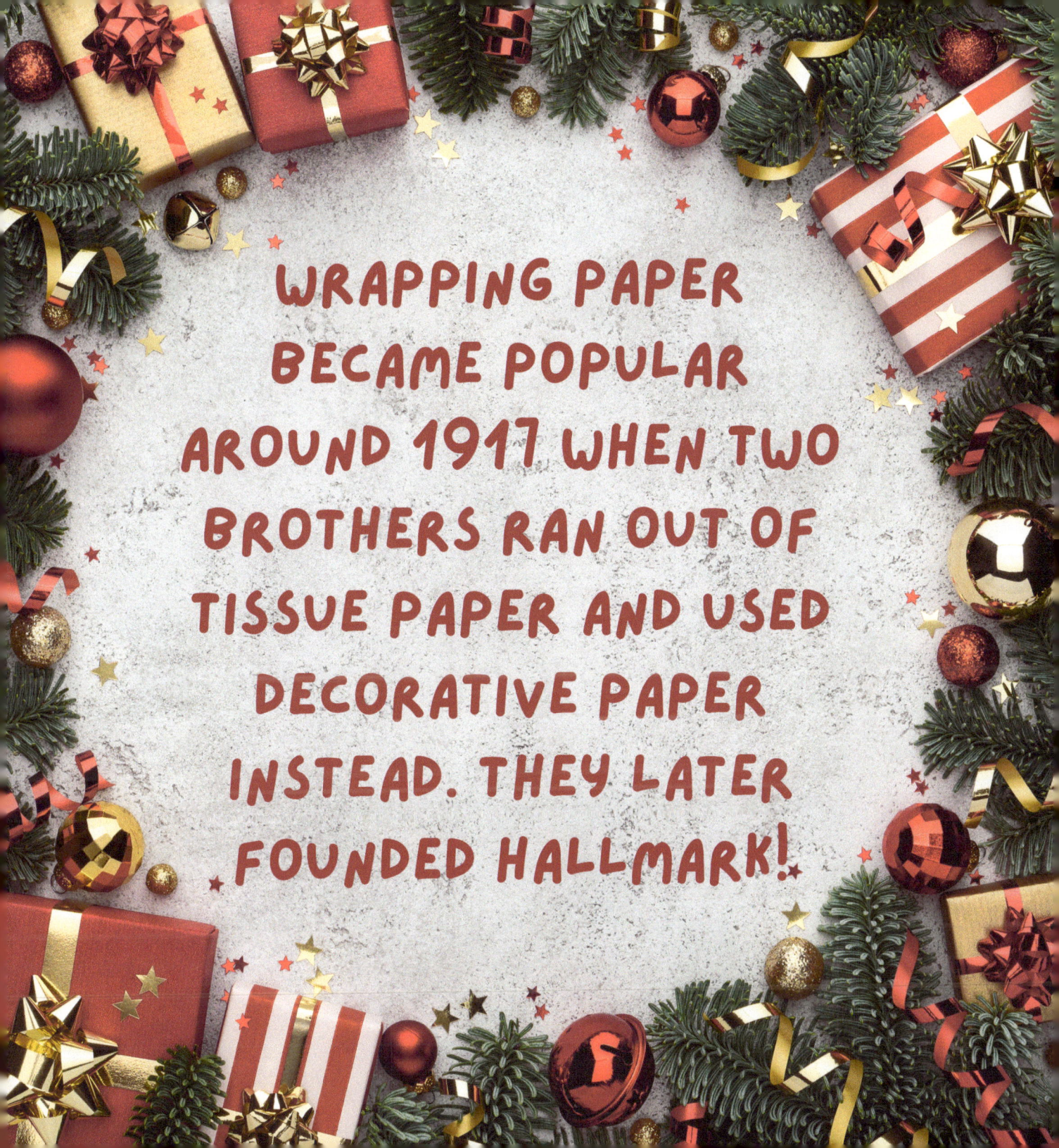

Wrapping paper became popular around 1917 when two brothers ran out of tissue paper and used decorative paper instead. They later founded Hallmark!

On Christmas Eve, in Iceland, it's common for people to exchange books as gifts. Then families often cozy up by the fire and spend the evening reading.

I love that idea.

There's a legend from old European folklore that animals can talk at midnight on Christmas Eve.

The NORAD Santa Tracker (run by the North American Aerospace Defense Command) has followed Santa's flight path every Christmas Eve since 1955.

And it all started because a young child called a misprinted phone number & got their hotline instead of a Santa hotline!

In parts of Europe, families hung their Christmas trees upside down to represent the Holy Trinity. Plus, it saved space in their small homes and kept the ornaments away from younger children.

When you sip eggnog, you're tasting a little bit of pirate history. Long ago, sailors and pirates drank it to celebrate on special days, especially around Christmas. A splash of rum kept it from spoiling on long voyages, and the creamy sweetness reminded them of home.

ARG

FUN FACT BOOKS
for Kids

COLLECT THEM ALL!

www.ingramcontent.com/pod-product-compliance
Lightning Source LLC
Chambersburg PA
CBHW041501220426
43661CB00016B/1216